One Day in the
DESERT

*Trophy Chapter Books by
Jean Craighead George:*

ONE DAY IN THE ALPINE TUNDRA
ONE DAY IN THE PRAIRIE
ONE DAY IN THE TROPICAL RAIN FOREST
ONE DAY IN THE WOODS

One Day in the
DESERT

by Jean Craighead George
illustrated by Fred Brenner

HarperTrophy®
A Division of HarperCollinsPublishers

One Day in the Desert
Text copyright © 1983 by Jean Craighead George
Illustrations copyright © 1983 by Fred Brenner
All rights reserved. No part of this book may be
used or reproduced in any manner whatsoever without
written permission except in the case of brief quotations
embodied in critical articles and reviews. Printed in
the United States of America. For information address
HarperCollins Children's Books, a division of HarperCollins
Publishers, 10 East 53rd Street, New York , NY 10022.

Library of Congress Cataloging-in-Publication Data
George, Jean Craighead, date
    One day in the desert.
    Summary: Explains how the animal and human inhabitants of the
Sonoran Desert of Arizona, including a mountain lion, a roadrunner, a
coyote, a tortoise, and members of the Papago Indian tribe, adapt to
and survive the desert's mercilesss heat.
    ISBN 0-690-04340-6. — ISBN 0-690-04341-4 (lib. bdg.)
    ISBN 0-06-442038-8 (pbk.)
    1. Desert ecology—Sonoran Desert—Juvenile literature.   2. Sonoran
Desert—Juvenile literature.   [1. Desert ecology.   2. Sonoran Desert.
3. Heat—Physiological effect.   4. Papago Indians.   5. Indians of North
America—Arizona.   6. Ecology.]   I. Brenner, Fred, ill.   II. title.
QH104.5.S58G46   1983   82-45924
591.5'2652'097917   CIP
                                                                     AC

❖
First Harper Trophy edition, 1996.
13 CG/OPM 40 39 38 37 36 35 34 33

One Day in the
DESERT

At daybreak on July 10th a mountain lion limped toward a Papago Indian hut, a small structure of grass and sticks on the bank of a dry river in the Sonoran Desert of Arizona. Behind it rose Mount Scorpion, a dark-red mountain. In all directions from the mountain stretched the gray-green desert. It was dry, hot and still.

The cactus wrens began to sing. The Gila woodpeckers squawked to each other across the hot air, arguing over their property lines. The kit foxes who

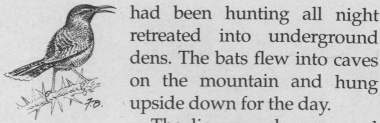 had been hunting all night retreated into underground dens. The bats flew into caves on the mountain and hung upside down for the day.

The lion was hungry and desperately thirsty. A poacher's bullet had torn into the flesh of his paw, and for two weeks he had lain in his den halfway up the mountain nursing his feverish wound. As the sun arose this day, he got to his feet. He must eat and drink.

The desert stretched below him. He paused and looked down upon the dry river called an arroyo. It was empty of water, but could be a raging torrent in the rainy season after a storm. He twisted his ears forward. A Papago Indian girl, Bird

Wing, and her mother were walking along the bank of the dry river. They entered the hut.

The lion smelled their scent on the air and limped toward them. He was afraid of people, but this morning he was desperate.

Six feet (1.8 meters) in length, he

stood almost 3 feet (a meter) tall. His fur was reddish brown above and white beneath. A black mustache marked his face. The backs of his ears and the tip of his tail were also black.

He growled as he came down the mountain, which was a huge clinker thrown up from the basement of the earth by an ancient volcano. Near its summit were pools where beaver and fish lived in the desert and which the mountain lion normally visited to hunt and drink. But today he went down, for it took less energy than going up.

The rising sun burned down from

space, heating the rocks and the soil until they were hot even through the well-padded feet of the lion. He stood in the shade of a rock at 8 A.M. when the temperature reached 80° Fahrenheit (26.6° Celsius).

This day would be memorable. Bird Wing, her mother, the lion and many of the animals below Mount Scorpion would be affected by July 10th. Some would survive and some would not, for the desert is ruthless.

Chapter 2

The Sonoran Desert is one of four deserts marked by distinctive plants that make up the great North American Desert, which extends from central Mexico to almost the Canadian border. The North American Desert covers more than 500,000 square miles (1,300,000 square kilometers).

All of the four deserts have one thing in common—little rain. Less than 10 inches (24 centimeters) a year fall on the greater parts of these deserts. The temperatures, however, vary from below freezing to the low 120s F (about 50°C).

Each one is slightly different. The Great Basin desert of Oregon, California, Idaho, Nevada, Utah and Wyoming— the most northern and the coldest—is largely covered with sagebrush, a plant that has adapted to the dry cold.

The Mojave Desert of California is the smallest and driest, with less than 4 inches (10 centimeters) of rain a year. The teddy-bear cactus called cholla (choy-ya), a cactus so spiny it seems to have fur, dominates this desert.

The third, the Chihuahuan (chee-wa-wan) Desert, lies largely in Mexico. Only 10 percent of it is in the United States, in New Mexico, Arizona and Texas. On this desert the yuccas and agaves, or century plants, have adapted and grow abundantly, lending a special look to the land.

The fourth and most magnificent is the Sonoran Desert of Mexico and Arizona. Unlike the other deserts, it has two rainy

seasons—showers in March and deluges in July and August. The rains nourish magnificent plants that support a great variety of creatures. The outstanding plant in this desert is the giant saguaro cactus, a tall plant that resembles a telephone pole with upturned arms. All the cacti—the saguaro, barrel, teddy bear and prickly pear—are unique to North America. They have evolved nowhere else in the world.

The North American Desert is dry because it is robbed of rain by the Pacific coast mountains. The clouds coming in from the ocean strike the high cold peaks and dump most of their moisture on the western side of the mountains. Practically no rain reaches the eastern side, which is in what is called the "rain shadow" by scientists.

All deserts are lands of extremes: too

hot, too dry, too wet. Yet they abound with living things that have adjusted to these excesses. To fight dryness, plants store water in their tissues or drop their leaves to prevent evaporation from their broad surfaces. They also grow spines, which do not use much water and which cast shadows on the plant to protect it from the blazing sun. They thicken stems and leaves to hold water.

The animals adapt by seeking out cool microclimates, small shelters out of the terrible heat. The microclimates are burrows in the ground where it is cool, crevices and caves in rocks, or the shade. Because of the dryness, the thin desert air does not hold heat. Shady spots can be 20°F (11°C) cooler than out in the sun.

A few animals adapt to the harsh conditions by manufacturing water from the starch in the seeds they eat. The perky kangaroo rat is one of these. Others move in the cool of the night.

The coyote hunts in the dark, as do the deer, ringtailed "cat" (cacomistle), desert fox, raccoon and lion. The honeypot ant, on the other hand, has such a tough outer skeleton that it can walk in extremely hot sunshine.

Chapter 3

On July 10th the wounded mountain lion was forced to hunt in the heat of the day. He could not wait for darkness. He made his way slowly down the trail toward the Papago Indian hut.

By 9 A.M. he was above the dwelling on a mountain ledge. The temperature climbed another degree. He sought the shade of a giant saguaro cactus and lay down to rest.

The scent of lion reached the nose of a coyote who was cooling off under the dark embankment of the dry river not far

from the Papago Indian hut.
He lifted his head, flicked
his ears nervously and got
to his feet. He ran swiftly
into his burrow beneath the
roots of the ancient saguaro cactus that
grew beside the hut.

The huge cactus was over 100 years
old, stood 75 feet (22.5 meters) tall and
weighed more than 6 tons (5.5 metric
tons). The last of its watermelon-red fruits
were ripe and on the ground. Bird Wing
and her mother were going to gather
them and boil them in the water they had
carried in buckets from the village. The
fruit makes a sweet, nourishing syrup.

At 11 A.M. they stretched out on their
mats in the hut. It was much too hot to
work. The temperature had reached
112° F (44.4°C).

The old cactus was drying up in the
heat. It drew on the last of the water in
the reservoir inside its trunk and shrank
ever so slightly, for it could expand and

contract like an accordion.

The mountain lion's tongue was swollen from lack of moisture. He got to his feet again.

A roadrunner, a ground-dwelling bird with a spiny crest and a long neck and legs, saw the lion pass his shady spot in the grass. He sped down the mountain, over the riverbank and into the dry riverbed.

He stopped under the embankment where the coyote had been. There he lifted his feathers to keep cool. Bird feathers are perhaps the best protection from both heat and cold, for they form dead air space, and dead air is one of the best insulations.

The roadrunner passed a family of seven peccaries, piglike animals with coarse coats, tusks and almost no tails. They stay alive in the dry desert by eating the water-storing prickly pear cactus, spines and all.

14

They were now lying in the cool of the paloverde trees that grow in thickets. Like the pencil-straight ocotillo and almost all the desert leafy plants, the paloverdes drop their leaves when the desert is extremely hot and dry. On July 10th they began falling faster and faster.

The scent of the lion reached the old boar. He lifted his head and watched the great beast. The lion turned away from the peccary family and limped toward the Indian hut. All the pigs, big and little, watched him.

A warm moist wind that had been moving northwest across the Gulf of Mexico for a day and a night met a cold wind blowing east from the Pacific coast mountains. The hot and cold air collided not far from the Mexico-Arizona border and exploded into a chain of white clouds. The meeting formed a stiff wind.

It picked up the desert dust and carried it toward Mount Scorpion.

As the lion limped across the embankment under which the roadrunner was hiding, the air around him began to fill with dust.

Near the coyote den dwelled a tarantula, a spider almost as big as a man's fist and covered with furlike hairs. She looked like a long-legged bear, and she

was sitting near the top of her burrow, a shaft she had dug straight down into the ground. The hot desert air forced her to let go with all eight of her legs. She dropped to the bottom of her shaft, where the air was cooler. The spider survives the heat by digging underground and by hunting at night. The moist crickets and other insects she eats quench her thirst.

A headstand beetle felt the heat of the day and became uncomfortable. He stopped hunting in the grass and scurried into the entrance of the tarantula hole. He was not afraid of the spider, with her poison fangs that kill prey, but he was wary of her. Hearing the spider coming up her shaft to see who was there, the headstand beetle got ready to fend her off. He stood on his head, aimed his rear end and mixed chemicals in his abdomen. The tarantula rushed at him and lifted her fangs. The headstand beetle shot a blistering-hot stream of a quinonoid chemical at the spider. She

writhed and dropped to the bottom of her den. The headstand beetle hid under a grass plant by the tarantula's door.

The temperature rose several more degrees.

Chapter 4

At 12:30 P.M. a desert tortoise, who was protected from the heat by two unusually thick shells of bone, went on eating the fruit of a prickly pear cactus. He was never thirsty. The moisture from the plants he ate was stored in his enormous bladder, a reservoir of pure water that desert tortoises have devised over the ages to adapt themselves to the dry heat. The water cools the reptiles on the hottest days and refreshes them on the driest.

The temperature reached 117°F (47.2°C). At last the tortoise felt warm. He turned around and pushed up on his toes. On his short legs he walked to his burrow under the paloverde bushes where the peccaries hunched, their eyes focused on the lion.

Inside his burrow the tortoise came upon a cottontail rabbit who had taken refuge there out of the hot sun. The tortoise could not go on. The heat poured in, and to lower the temperature he plugged up the entrance with his back feet. On the ceiling above his head clung

a spiny-tailed lizard and a Texas banded gecko, reptiles who usually like the heat. At 12:30 P.M. on July 10th they sought the protection of the tortoise's burrow.

The temperature rose one more degree. A cactus wren who had sung at dawn slipped into her nest in a teddy-bear cactus at the edge of the paloverde thicket. She opened her beak to release heat.

The peccaries heard soft sounds like rain falling. Hundreds of small lizards who usually hunted the leaves of the paloverde, even on the hottest days, could no longer endure the high temperature. They were dropping to the ground and seeking shelter under sticks and stones.

A kangaroo rat was in her labyrinth

under the leafless, pencil-like ocotillo plants. She awakened when the temperature reached 119°F (47.3°C). Her bedroom near the surface of the  desert floor had become uncomfortably hot. Her body was drying out. She scurried along a tunnel, turned a corner and ran down a slope toward a room under the giant saguaro cactus. She paused at her pantry to eat seeds of the mesquite tree before retiring to the cool, deep chamber. While she slept, her internal system converted the starch of the seeds into water and revived her dry body.

Chapter 5

The lion walked into the paloverde bushes. The peccaries squealed in fright and trotted out into the terrible sunshine. In a cloud of dust they sped into the dry riverbed and frightened the roadrunner. He ran out from under the overhang and flew into the saguaro forest on the far side of the dry river. The pigs hid under the embankment where the roadrunner had been.

The injured lion could not chase the peccaries. He lifted his head, smelled the sweet piglets and climbed up the Indian trail till he was at the hut. Bird Wing and

24

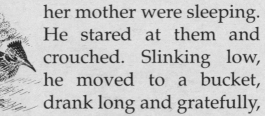

her mother were sleeping. He stared at them and crouched. Slinking low, he moved to a bucket, drank long and gratefully, then lay down in the doorway of the hut.

The temperature climbed one more degree. The birds stopped singing. Even the cicadas, who love hot weather and drum louder and faster in the heat, could no longer endure the fiery temperature. They stopped making sounds with their feet and wings and sat still. The Gila woodpecker flew into his hole in the giant saguaro. Below him, in one

of his old nests, sat the sparrow-sized elf owl. He opened his beak and lifted his feathers.

Bird Wing was awakened by thirst. She tipped one of the water buckets and drank deeply. The desert was so quiet she became alarmed.

Clouds were racing toward Mount Scorpion. They were black and purple. Constant flashes of lightning illuminated them from within. She crept to the back of the hut and lay down beside her mother. She closed her eyes.

At 1:20 P.M. the temperature reached 121°F (49.4°C).

This hour on July 10th was the hottest hour on record at the bottom of Mount Scorpion.

Even the well-insulated honeypot ants could not tolerate the temperature. They ran toward the entrance of their labyrinth near a pack rat nest by the hut. Some managed to get underground in the caverns where sister ants hung from the ceilings. Forager honeypot ants store the sweets from plants they have gathered in the bellies of hanging ants, some of which become as round as balloons and as big as marbles. The last two foraging ants ran across the hot soil to get home. They shriveled and died in seconds.

The peccaries under the embankment dug into the earth to find coolness.

Chapter 6

The clouds covered the sun.

Instantly, the temperature dropped four degrees.

The tortoise shoveled more dirt into the mouth of his burrow.

The thunder boomed like Indian drums.

The kangaroo rat felt the earth tremble. She ran to her door, smelled rain on the air and scurried to a U-shaped tunnel. She went down it and up to a room at the top. There she tucked her nose into her groin to sleep.

The temperature dropped five more

 degrees. A rattlesnake came out of the pack rat's nest and slid back to his hunting spot at the rear of the hut. The cicadas sang again. The cactus wren looked out of the entrance of her ball nest in the teddy-bear cactus.

A thunderclap exploded sharply. Bird Wing awoke. She saw the lion stretched in the doorway. She took her mother's arm and shook her gently until she awoke. Signaling her to be quiet, she pointed to the mountain lion. Bird Wing's mother parted the grass at the

rear of the hut and, after pushing Bird Wing out, backed out herself.

The rattlesnake buzzed a warning.

The sky darkened. Lightning danced from saguaro cactus to saguaro cactus. Bird Wing's mother looked at the clouds and the dry arroyo.

"We must get out of here," she said. "Follow me up the mountain." They scrambled over the rocks on hands and feet without looking back.

Huge raindrops splattered onto the dust. Bird Wing and her mother reached an overhanging rock on the mountain.

Lightning flashed around them like white horsewhips.

The thunder cracked and boomed. Then water gushed out of the sky. The rain fell in such torrents that Bird Wing and her mother could not see the dry river, the hut or the old saguaro. They sat quietly, waiting and listening.

A flash of lightning shot out of a cloud and hit the old saguaro cactus. It smoked, split and fell to the ground. The elf owl flew into the downpour. His wings and body became so wet, he soared down to the grass beneath the paloverde bushes. The woodpecker stayed where he was, bracing himself with his stiff tail.

The crash of the saguaro terrified the coyote. He darted out of his den under the tree and back to the dry riverbed. The peccaries dug deeper into the embankment. The roadrunner took to his feet and ran up the slope beyond the giant saguaro forest.

Chapter 7

The rain became torrents, the torrents became waterfalls and the waterfalls cascaded out of the sky until all the moisture was wrung from the clouds. They drizzled and stopped giving rain. The storm clouds rumbled up the canyon above the dry riverbed.

The sun came out. Bird Wing and her mother did not move. They listened. The desert rocks dripped and the cacti crackled softly as they swelled with water. Cactus roots lie close to the surface, spreading out from the plants in all directions to absorb every possible drop of water. The

34

roots send the water up into the trunks and barrels and pads to be stored.

A drumroll sounded up Scorpion Pass.

The peccaries heard it and darted out from under the embankment. They struggled up the bank and raced into the saguaro forest.

The lion got to his feet. He limped through the door.

The coyote rushed out of the dry riverbed. The wet elf owl hooked his beak around a twig of a paloverde and pulled himself upward toward higher limbs.

Water came bubbling and singing down the arroyo. It filled the riverbed from bank to bank, then rose like a great cement wall, a flash flood that filled the canyon. It swept over the embankment, over the hut, over the old saguaro cactus. It rose higher, thundered into the paloverdes and roared over the rocks at the foot of the mountain. It boomed into the valley, spread out and disappeared into the dry earth.

The coyote was washed out from under the embankment. He tumbled head over heels, swam to the surface and climbed onto an uprooted mass of prickly pears. On this he sailed into the valley and was dropped safely onto the outwash plain when the water went into the ground.

Stunned, he shook himself and looked around. Before him the half-drowned pack rat struggled. Recovering his wits, the coyote pounced upon him.

The lion was lifted up by the flood
and thrown against a clump of ocotillo.
He clung to it for a moment, then, too
weak to struggle, slipped beneath the
water.

Chapter 8

The flash flood that had trickled, then roared, trickled and then was gone. The banks of the arroyo dripped. Bird Wing and her mother walked to the spot where their hut had been. There was no sign of house, pack rat nest, saguaro, or lion.

"But for the lion, we would be dead," said Bird Wing. "We must thank him." She faced the mountain and closed her eyes for a moment. Her mother picked up an ocotillo stick and turned it over in her hand.

"We will rebuild our house up the mountain above the flood line," she said. Bird Wing nodded vigorously and gathered sticks, too.

The kangaroo rat sat in her room above the U trap that had stopped the water from reaching her. She waited until the floodwaters seeped into the ground. Then she began to repair her labyrinth.

The peccaries came out of the saguaro forest and rooted for insects among the billions of seeds that had been dumped on the land by the flood. The land was greening, the sky was blue. The roadrunner came back to the saguaro forest, ran down a young snake and ate it.

The cactus wren and owl did not call. The rattlesnake did not rattle. They had not survived the wrath of the desert on this day, July 10th.

Bird Wing walked to the arroyo edge. The earth trembled at her feet. She looked down. Plugs of sand popped out of the wet bank like corks. In each hole sat a grinning spadefoot toad, creatures who must grow up in the water. Then what were they doing in the desert? Waiting for just this moment.

They hopped into the brilliant sunshine and leaped into the puddles in the arroyo. Quickly they mated, quickly they laid eggs and quickly they ate and dug backward into the sand with the spades on their feet. Far underground their skins secreted a sticky gelatin that would prevent them from drying up. In this manner they survived in the hot waterless desert.

The warm sunlight of late afternoon heated the water in the puddles, speed-

ing up the development of the toad eggs. They must hatch into pollywogs and change into toads before the blazing heat dried up the puddles.

At 7:33 P.M. soft blue and purple light swept over the beautiful desert. In the puddles pollywogs swam.

Bibliography

Baylor, Byrd. *Desert Voices*. New York: Scribner, 1981.

Epstein, Samuel. *All About the Desert*. New York: Random House, 1957.

Graham, Ada. *The Changing Desert*. San Francisco: Sierra Club Books, 1981.

Gray, Robert. *Cougar: The Natural Life of a North American Mountain Lion*. New York: W. W. Norton, 1972.

Johnson, Sylvia A. *Animals of the Deserts*. Minneapolis: Lerner Publications Company, 1976.

Leopold, A. Starker. *The Desert*. New York: Time-Life Books, 1961.

Montgomery, Rutherford G. *King of the Castle: The Story of a Kangaroo Rat*. Cleveland and New York: The World Publishing Company, 1961.

Pitt, Valerie, and David Cook. *A Closer Look at Deserts*. New York: Franklin Watts, 1975.

Pond, Alonzo. *Deserts, Silent Lands of the World*. New York: W. W. Norton, 1965.

Posell, Elsa Z. *Deserts*. Chicago: Children's Press, 1982.

Young, Donald. *The Great American Desert*. New York: Julian Messner, 1980.

Index

Numbers in *italics* refer to illustrations.

47

Don't miss this *One Day* chapter book:

One Day in the WOODS

by Jean Craighead George
illustrated by Gary Allen

There's a wizard hiding in the Teatown Woods, and Rebecca is determined to find it. Her uncle has told her about the beautiful ovenbird, "wizard of the woods," and she thinks it must be magic.

But when Rebecca sets out into the forest, she never expects to find magic everywhere she looks. A squirrel flies through the air. A deer vanishes before her eyes. And the mysterious ovenbird holds the greatest surprise of all. . . .

Published by Harper Trophy Paperback Books

Don't miss this *One Day* chapter book:

One Day in the TROPICAL RAIN FOREST

by Jean Craighead George
illustrated by Gary Allen

It is dawn, and young Tepui makes his way through the rain forest. He treasures his homeland and all of its wildlife, from the giant trees to the playful monkeys to the colorful treetop birds.

But today is doomsday for Tepui's rain forest. Eleven bulldozers and four trucks will soon arrive to level the forest. Tepui is desperate to stop them, and there's just one way to do it. He must discover a butterfly no one has ever seen—by the end of the day.

Published by Harper Trophy Paperback Books

Don't miss this *One Day* chapter book:

One Day in the PRAIRIE
by Jean Craighead George
illustrated by Bob Marstall

Henry Rush is spending the day at the Prairie Wildlife Refuge, determined to photograph a prairie dog doing a back flip. But while he watches and waits at the edge of prairie dog town, he fails to notice the electricity humming through the air. Or the buffalo anxiously pawing at the ground. Or the purple-blue cloud building over the prairie grass.

A tornado is forming in the west. And when the dark funnel touches down, it will wipe out everything in its path . . .

Published by Harper Trophy Paperback Books